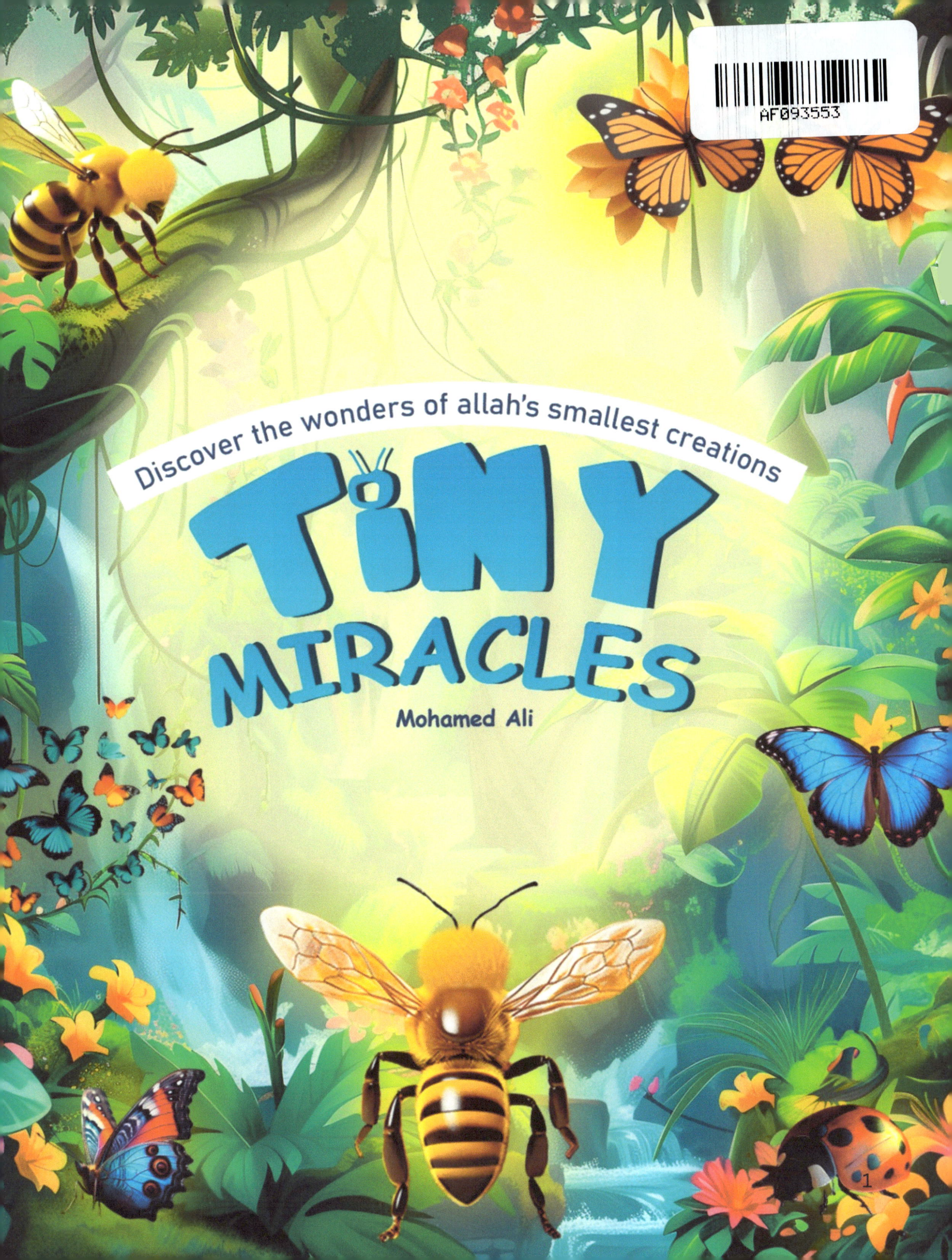

Copyright © 2024 by Mohamed Ali

All rights reserved. No part of this book may be reproduced, stored in a retrieval system, or transmitted in any form or by any means—whether electronic or mechanical—without prior written permission from the author, except for brief quotations used in reviews or critical articles.

ISBN: 979-8-9917389-6-5

Published by: M. Publishing

First Edition

Printed in the USA

All praise is due to Allah, the Creator of all things.

Dedication

To the curious hearts and wondering minds of children everywhere. May you always see the beauty in the smallest of creatures and marvel at Allah's extraordinary design.

And to parents, teachers, and caregivers. Thank you for nurturing curiosity, sharing knowledge, and guiding young explorers through the wonders of creation.

This book is for you.

INTRODUCTION

Have you ever taken a moment to reflect on the incredible wonders of the tiny creatures around you? Though they may seem small and insignificant, they are brimming with extraordinary miracles that play a vital role in our ecosystem.

These remarkable little beings help maintain the delicate balance of our world in numerous ways. They nurture and support the growth of plants, ensuring lush landscapes and thriving gardens. They tirelessly work to clean our earth, breaking down waste and recycling nutrients into the soil.

They also serve as a crucial source of animal nourishment, offering sustenance to countless species while protecting and preserving nature's intricate tapestry.

Even beyond their immediate roles in the ecosystem, these tiny wonders inspire us, sparking our creativity and connection to the natural world.

In this book, we embark on a journey to uncover the miracles these small yet mighty creatures brought forth—those tiny "its" that contribute to the beauty of life around us.

But hold on! There's a playful challenge awaiting you! Before you can meet each one of these tiny miracle-makers, you'll need to solve a riddle. Each riddle will offer clues about a particular miracle, culminating in the question: "Guess Who I Am?"

Are you ready to explore, learn, and marvel at the enchanting world of Allah's tiny miracles?

HOW TO PLAY THIS RIDDLE BOOK

RIDDLE

This activity can be enjoyed individually, in pairs, or small groups. Here's how:

1. The Questioner: One person will take on the role of the Questioner and read aloud the riddle in the top green section.
2. Read Clearly: Make sure everyone listens carefully to the riddle. If someone doesn't hear or understand, feel free to repeat it.
3. Pause and Think: Give everyone a moment to pause, wonder, and guess the answer. No rushing—let curiosity guide the way!
4. Share Your Guess: Encourage participants to share their guesses before revealing the answer.

REVEAL

Once everyone has made their guess, the Questioner reveals the answer by reading reveal section.

STORY

After revealing the answer, read this story section together to learn about the insect's miracle and its role in Allah's creation.

Look closely at the illustration on the next page, paying attention to every detail. Let it fill your heart with wonder and your mind with gratitude for these small yet extraordinary creatures.

Remember: This is a fun, thoughtful activity. Take your time, enjoy each riddle, and celebrate every discovery!

1. BUZZING HELPER

RIDDLE

I dance through gardens, flying from bloom to bloom, carrying fine golden dust upon my tiny legs.

With each delicate visit, I help create juicy fruits and produce a delightful treat just for you.

That is my remarkable gift.

Guess Who I Am?

REVEAL

"I am a bee!"

STORY

My extraordinary gift is the art of pollination! As I journey from flower to flower, I carry pollen, enabling plants to grow their delicious fruits and seeds. In addition, I work tirelessly to create sweet, golden honey, a delicacy for you to relish.

Bestowed with this vital role by Allah, I spread sweetness and nurture life all around the globe.

"I am a bee! a chief pollinator".

"We are honey producers."

2. LITTLE BUILDER

RIDDLE

I burrow deep beneath the surface, uncovering small precious gems in the soil.

Alongside my devoted comrades, I labor tirelessly to create something extraordinary.

This is the wonder we achieve together.

Can you guess who I am?"

REVEAL

"I am an ant!"

STORY

My wonder lies in the strength of teamwork! My fellow compatriots and I collaborate harmoniously to construct elaborate homes and keep our environment pristine.

Though Allah made us small, our impact is immense. Let this remind you of the vital importance of unity and cooperation in achieving great things.

"We move bigger objects as a team!"

"We show you the importance of teamwork!"

3. COLORFUL DANCER

RIDDLE

I dance gracefully through blooming gardens, my delicate wings shimmering with the vibrant colors of a thousand rainbows. I gently alight on blossoms, sipping their sweet nectar and bestowing a precious gift upon the world.

That is my miracle.

Can you guess who I am?"

REVEAL

"I am a butterfly!"

STORY

My miracle lies in the enchanting dance of pollination, where I nurture the growth of plants while infusing joy into the world with my vivid, colorful wings.

Each flutter reflects the exquisite artistry of Allah, manifesting beauty and life in every moment of my journey.

"I taste my food just by stepping on it!"

"Imagine if you could taste your food just by stepping on it!"

4. NIGHT LANTERN

RIDDLE

In the heart of warm summer nights, I shimmer like a tiny star scattered across the dark sky. My soft, glowing light is a secret language, allowing me to communicate with those I hold dear.

That is my miracle.

Can you guess who I am?"

REVEAL

"I am a firefly!"

STORY

My miracle is bioluminescence—a magical light that glows in the night, guiding me to my fellow fireflies. With this enchanting shine, I dance in the darkness, connecting with my companions.

It's a beautiful reminder of Allah's boundless creativity, lighting up the world with wonder and awe.

"I am a firefly!"

"I use my glowing abdomen to send signals, like flashing secret messages in the dark!"

5. EARTH CLEANER

RIDDLE

I skillfully gather what many believe undesirable, shaping it into something valuable and vital for life.

My diligent work ensures that the earth remains clean and vibrant.

I am nature's miraculous recycler.

Can you guess who I am?

REVEAL

"I am a dung beetle!"

STORY

My miracle lies in my ability to recycle waste! With great care, I collect animal droppings and transform them into nutrient-rich resources that enrich the soil.

Created by Allah as nature's diligent cleaner, I play a crucial role in promoting the health and strength of plants, ensuring a thriving ecosystem.

"I am a master recycler!"

"I roll and bury waste, turning it into food and fertilizer."

6. SPOTTED PROTECTOR

RIDDLE

I delight in feasting on the tiny pests that jeopardize plants' vitality and the crops' richness. Adorned with a vibrant, polka-dotted shell, I resemble a little hero, bravely patrolling the garden.

With every bite I take, I unleash a miracle, nurturing the very essence of nature while safeguarding the flourishing life around me.

Can you guess who I am?

REVEAL

"I am a ladybug!"

STORY

My miracle lies in my role as a guardian of greenery! I diligently protect plants by devouring the harmful insects that seek to destroy them.

Created by Allah as a small yet mighty helper, I serve as a reminder that even the tiniest creatures play a vital role in maintaining the balance of our ecosystems, enriching gardens and farms alike.

"I am a ladybug!"

"I chew on troublesome insects like aphids, protecting plants and helping gardens thrive."

7. SKY HUNTER

RIDDLE

I dart through the sky with delicate wings that glisten in the sunlight.

I feast on the annoying bugs that complicate your outdoor moments.

It is my unique gift to the world.

Can you guess who I am?

REVEAL

"I am a dragonfly!"

STORY

My gift is hunting mosquitoes and other pesky insects. I keep their numbers in check with remarkable speed and agility, creating a healthier environment for all.

My role in maintaining nature's balance is a beautiful miracle, a testament to Allah's wisdom and perfect design.

"I am dragonfly."

"A sky hunter of mosquitoes and other pesky insects with ease."

8. GREEN JUMPER

RIDDLE

I bound across sun-kissed fields, my powerful legs propelling me into the air.

As I dance among the blades of grass, I create a joyful melody that fills the warm summer breeze.

I am a symbol of nature's wonder.

Can you guess who I am?

REVEAL

"I am a grasshopper!"

STORY

My miracle is aerating the earth and enriching the soil as I gracefully leap with my strong legs. My cheerful chirps add harmony to nature's symphony, reminding everyone of life's simple joys.

Allah created me as a joyful jumper, bringing happiness to the vibrant meadows.

"I am a grasshopper."

"I help mix the soil and bring life to the land."

9. SILENT HUNTER

RIDDLE

I stand motionless, my limbs delicately folded like a prayer, ever vigilant for the opportune moment to strike.

I silently intercept the pesky insects that threaten the vitality of the surrounding plants.

This is the miraculous nature of my existence.

Can you unravel my identity?"

REVEAL

"I am a praying mantis!"

STORY

My miracle is patience and precision in hunting! With swift movements, I protect gardens by devouring harmful pests. Allah crafted me as an astute hunter, teaching the value of waiting and acting with wisdom.

In my world, every moment counts, and observation leads to success.

"I am praying mantis."

"I'm always in prayer, reminding you to be obedient."

10. TINY DRINKER

RIDDLE

I fly through the moonlit night, humming softly in your ear.
Though I sip on the nectar of life, I also play a crucial role in sustaining other creatures.

This is my miracle.

Can you unravel the mystery of my existence?"

REVEAL

"I am a mosquito!"

STORY

My miracle is my vital role in the food chain. Though I may seem a nuisance, I provide essential sustenance for birds, bats, and fish.

Allah created me as a small yet indispensable creature, showing that even the tiniest beings play a crucial role in nature's balance.

"I am a mosquito. I serve as food for birds, bats, and fish, helping keep the food chain balanced."

"There is a fish called Gambusia affinis that lives off me"

11. WOOD RECYCLER

RIDDLE

I gnaw through sturdy wood, crafting towering structures alongside my family members.

I transform lifeless trees into valuable materials that nourish the earth.

This is my extraordinary gift.

Can you guess who I am?

REVEAL

"I am a termite!"

STORY

My extraordinary gift is the art of recycling wood! I take what is old and seemingly useless, breathe new life into it, enrich the soil, and pave the way for vibrant plant life to thrive.

Created by Allah, I serve as a natural recycler, embodying the powerful concept of renewal and showing the beauty in transformation.

"I am a termite"

"I am a tiny building engineer!"

12. THREAD MAKER

RIDDLE

I weave delicate, shimmering threads that humans hold dear.

For millennia, my precious gift has been celebrated and admired. This is the marvel I create.

Can you guess who I am?

REVEAL

"I am a silk moth!"

STORY

My miracle is silk! With my soft, lustrous threads, I bring an essence of beauty and comfort to your lives.

It is a divine blessing bestowed upon me by Allah, allowing me to share the wonders of creation with you.

"I am a silk moth"

"I am a tiny silk artist!"

13. WEB WEAVER

RIDDLE

I skillfully spin delicate, silky threads to craft something remarkably strong.

With my intricate traps, I ensnare my prey as I tirelessly weave throughout the day.

This is my extraordinary gift.

Can you guess who I am?

REVEAL

"I am a spider!"

STORY

My miracle is weaving intricate webs with silk, one of nature's strongest materials. I use it to capture prey and survive, and humans study my silk for innovative creations.

Allah gifted me this unique talent, showcasing patience and creativity in His extraordinary design.

"I am a spider, a master weaver!"

"My web is both my home and my food trap"

14. WATER STRIDER

RIDDLE

I glide effortlessly over the water's shimmering surface, my legs so delicate and light.

In the warm glow of sunlight, I dance across ponds, leaving barely a ripple in my wake.

This is my miracle.

Can you guess who I am?"

REVEAL

"I am a water strider!"

STORY

My miracle is my ability to walk on water! My specially designed legs distribute my weight, keeping me from sinking. I bring the water's surface to life as I glide across ponds and streams.

Allah created me as a reminder that nothing is impossible through His wisdom.

"I am a water strider"

"I can walk on water without sinking".

15. CARPENTER

RIDDLE

I burrow deep within the heart of timber, weaving intricate pathways as I go.

My tireless craftsmanship transforms mighty trees into nutrient-rich soil, facilitating nature's grand design.

This is the wonder I bring.

Can you uncover my identity?

REVEAL

"I am a bark beetle!"

STORY

My miracle is recycling wood! I carve intricate tunnels into trees, breaking them down so they can nourish the earth again. My work supports the circle of life, sustaining forests.

Allah gifted me this essential role, showing how every creature contributes to nature's grand design.

"I am a bark beetle"

"I carve tunnels inside trees, breaking down dead wood and returning nutrients to the soil"

A bark beetle

16. LEAF MIMIC

RIDDLE

I look like a twig or a branch, so thin,

I hide in plain sight, and you can't see me begin.

This is my miracle.

Guess Who I Am?

REVEAL

"I am a stick insect!"

STORY

My miracle is camouflage! I blend perfectly with leaves and branches, keeping myself safe from predators.

Allah gave me the gift of disguise, reminding you that protection comes in many forms.

"I am stick insect"

"I blend perfectly with branches and leaves, staying hidden from predators".

17. GOLDEN DIGGER

RIDDLE

I work with my family in a home of gold,

Storing treasures in shapes so bold.

This is my miracle.

Guess Who I Am?

REVEAL

"I am a Honeybee Drone!"

STORY

My miracle is teamwork and building! My family and I work together to create honeycombs, storing honey for us and you.

Allah gave us precision and unity, teaching you how teamwork builds greatness.

"I am a honeybee drone"

"We tend to drone cells"

18. ACROBAT HUNTER

RIDDLE

I leap through the air without a sound,

With sharp little eyes, my prey is found.

This is my miracle.

Guess Who I Am?

REVEAL

"I am a Jumping Spider!"

STORY

My miracle is my incredible vision and acrobatics! I can jump many times my body length to catch my prey.

Allah made me agile and sharp-eyed, showing you that size doesn't define strength.

"I am a jumping spider"

"I leap great distances to catch my prey"

19. SAND ARTIST

RIDDLE

I dig in the sand and make a trap so neat,

I wait for my dinner to slide to my feet.

This is my miracle.

Guess Who I Am?

REVEAL

"I am a Antlion!"

STORY

My miracle is my sandy trap! I dig cone-shaped pits in the sand to catch my prey.

Allah gave me patience and precision, reminding you that cleverness can outsmart strength.

"I am an antlion"

" I dig cone-shaped pits in the sand to catch unsuspecting prey".

20. SILENT SONGSTER

RIDDLE

My music fills the night with a gentle tune,

I hide in the grass under the moon.

This is my miracle.

Guess Who I Am?

REVEAL

"I am a Cricket!"

STORY

My miracle is my song! I rub my wings together to create music in the night, calling out to my friends.

Allah gave me this gentle voice to remind you that even the quietest sounds have meaning.

"I am a cricket"

"I create a soothing chirping song that fills the evening air"

CREATE YOUR RIDDLE

Use this prompt to guide your writing:

"Think about what your insect does. How would you describe its miracle?"

Example:

"I buzz from flower to flower, collecting something sweet.
Without my help, your fruits wouldn't be a treat."

"Guess Who I Am?"

Now it's your turn! Write your riddle below:

My Riddle:

The Answer:

My insect is a: _____

Illustrate Your Insect:

Draw a picture of your insect below. Add fun details like where it lives or what it's doing!

INSECT OBSERVATION JOURNAL

Activity:

Become a Nature Explorer! Grab your journal and head outside to your backyard, garden, park, or schoolyard. Look closely—insects buzzing, crawling, or flying all around.

How to Use Your Insect Journal:

1. Find an Insect: Look carefully under leaves, near flowers, or on tree branches.
2. Draw It: You can use the space below to draw the insect you found.
3. What is it doing? Write down what your insect was doing (e.g., flying, eating, building a home).
4. Reflect: Think about your discovery and answer this question:
5. "What did you learn from watching this insect?"

My Insect Journal Page:

Date: _____

Where I found it: _____

Draw Your Insect:

What was the insect doing?

What did I learn from watching this insect?

CLOSING REFLECTION

This book explores the amazing things about some of Earth's smallest creatures, from bees to praying mantis and the silk moth. These creatures remind us that every small creation is vital to balance our world.

The praying mantis teaches us about patience and wisdom. It waits calmly for the right moment to strike, helping to protect gardens from pests. This shows Allah's wisdom in creating a strategic and purposeful hunter.

The silk moth also shows Allah's creativity. A simple caterpillar transforms into one of the world's most valuable materials—silk. People have valued and used this gift from a tiny worm that weaves its cocoon for thousands of years.

These examples show just a tiny part of the many creatures in our world. Each one plays a vital role with care and precision, all part of Allah's grand design.

The Quran says, "Indeed, in the creation of the heavens and the earth and the alternation of the night and the day are signs for those of understanding." (Quran 3:190).

This verse invites us to think, watch, and appreciate the beauty and balance in everything around us.

GLOSSARY

Bioluminescence: Some animals, like fireflies, can create light from their bodies.

Builder: An insect (termite), that uses natural materials to construct homes.

Camouflage: The ability to blend into the surroundings to stay hidden from predators or prey.

Cocoon: A protective covering spun by insect larvae, like the silk moth, to stay safe during transformation.

Drone: A male honeybee whose main job is to support the queen bee and help the hive thrive.

Ecosystem: A community of plants, animals, and insects living in a balanced environment.

Hive: A home for bees where they store honey and care for their young.

Hunter: An insect that catches and eats other insects, like the praying mantis or jumping spider.

Miracle: Something extraordinary, like the bioluminescent glow of a firefly.

Nectar: A sweet liquid found in flowers that insects, like bees and butterflies, love to drink.

Pollen: A yellow powder found in flowers that insects carry from one flower to another to help plants grow fruits and seeds.

Pollination: Transferring pollen from one flower to another allows plants to produce seeds and fruits.

Predator: An animal or insect that hunts and eats other insects, like the praying mantis.

Recycle: The process of breaking down materials to be used again, like how the bark beetle recycles wood.

Reflections: Thoughts or observations made after watching and learning from nature.

Silk: A strong, soft thread made by insects like the silk moth and spider.

Spinneret: A part of a spider's body that produces silk threads for webs.

Web: A net-like structure made by spiders using silk threads to catch prey.

www.ingramcontent.com/pod-product-compliance
Lightning Source LLC
LaVergne TN
LVHW070439070526
838199LV00036B/670